MINECRAFT

MASTER BUILDER

MONSTERS

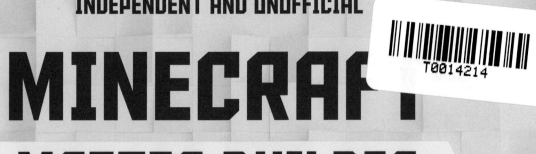

T0014214

MINECRAFT

MONSTERS

MORTIMER

CONTENTS

06   **WELCOME TO MINECRAFT MONSTERS**

08   **HERALDIC BEASTS**
10   PHOENIX
12   GRIFFIN
16   MANTICORE

24   **NORSE MONSTERS**
26   FENRIR WOLF
28   KRAKEN
32   THE WORLD SERPENT

38   **GREEK MYTHS**
40   CYCLOPS
42   MINOTAUR
46   CERBERUS

KRAKEN

MINOTAUR

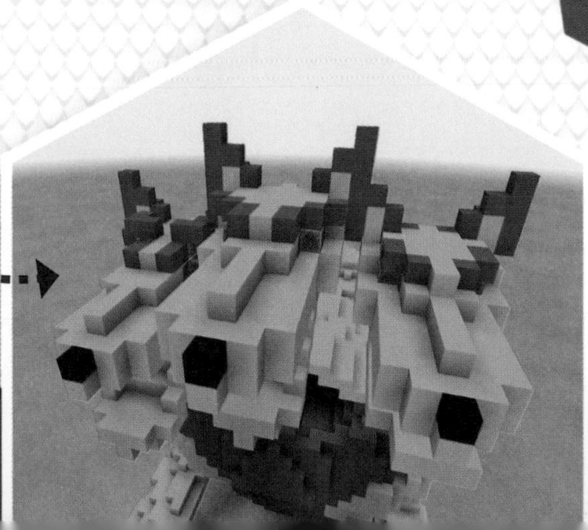

CERBERUS

YETI

CHIMERA ·····

54   AROUND THE WORLD
56   KAPPA
58   YETI
62   SPHINX

68   EPIC SHOWDOWNS
70   CHIMERA

SPHINX

FENRIR WOLF

WELCOME TO MINECRAFT
《 MONSTERS 》

From griffins to centaurs, and sea monsters to humanoids, this book is packed with the most awesome monsters imaginable. Tales of these mythical creatures have been around for centuries and remain popular today. We've heard the story of the phoenix rising from the ashes, and the famous yeti or cyclops, and now it's your chance to build them all!

《 NEW TO MINECRAFT? 》

If you STILL haven't played Minecraft yet, then prepare to have your mind blown! We recommend getting to know how everything works before going any further. Just download the game and have a good play around. The more you know about Minecraft and how it works, the easier it will be for you to tackle the builds in this book!

YETI

In the folklore of Nepal, the **Yeti** or **Abominable Snowman** is an ape-like creature, taller than an average human.

⟪ BEFORE YOU GET STARTED! ⟫

This book is divided into four sections. The step-by-step builds have lots of handy hints with illustrated instructions that help make it easy to follow. These builds are either easy, medium or master level. It's best to start with the simple ones first and work your way up to the more challenging monsters!

⟪ DOING MORE ⟫

This guide can help you to master your building skills, from beginner to total pro! Once you've got to grips with the monsters in this book, you can let your imagination lead the way. How about designing and building your own monsters? Experiment using different blocks to see what awesome things you can create.

STAYING SAFE ONLINE

We all know that Minecraft is heaps of fun, but it is important that you know how to stay safe online. Follow these tips to remind you to be safe when you play!

- ☐ ALWAYS tell a trusted adult what you're doing and ask before downloading anything
- ☐ speak to a trusted adult if you are worried about anything
- ☐ find a child-friendly server
- ☐ watch out for viruses and malware
- ☐ turn off chat
- ☐ only screen share with real-life friends
- ☐ set a time limit for game-play

LOCH NESS MONSTER

TROLL

In Norse mythology, **trolls** are ugly giants called jötnar. They turn to stone in the sunlight. Some of them have a single eye.

In Scottish folklore, the **Loch Ness Monster,** or **'Nessie',** is a creature said to inhabit Loch Ness, a loch in the Scottish Highlands.

HERALDIC
« BEASTS »

Up first we have the epic heraldic beasts. The creatures on these pages have featured throughout history as symbols on shields and armour. Here we'll introduce you to everything from the unicorn to the phoenix.

« BASILISK »

The basilisk is an unusual-looking monster – it's a mix between a rooster and a serpent. It is sometimes known as a cockatrice. According to legend, the basilisk could kill with a mere glance or a breath. The only known thing to out-smart the basilisk was the humble weasel, which was thought to have a deadly venom as defence.

« GRIFFIN »

The griffin, or griffon, is part eagle and part lion and is mostly shown with wings, but not always! Griffins appear in the mythology of many ancient cultures. In Greek mythology, they symbolised strength and wisdom. Greedy griffins were believed to collect and guard gold.

A **Griffin** has a bird's head, which is often an eagle.

The **basilisk** has large wings and the power to kill with a glance. Yikes!

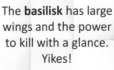

MANTICORE

The manticore has the body of a lion and the tail of a scorpion. Some describe the beast as having a tail covered in venomous spines that could be fired off like weapons. In medieval times, the manticore was thought to represent the devil.

The **Manticore** makes a trumpet sound to communicate.

WYVERN

The desert-dwelling wyvern is part dragon and part lizard, and features on European coats of arms. Unlike a dragon, it has two legs rather than four. This fire-breathing monster has a spiny tail and is an excellent hunter. Yep, you don't want to get on the wrong side of one of these guys!

UNICORN

This elegant, horse-like creature is easy to spot with the horn on top of its head. The unicorn is a symbol of purity and power in Celtic mythology. It is described as being a wild and strong creature. Scotland's national animal is a unicorn, as seen on the royal coat of arms.

PHOENIX

This fiery, eagle-sized bird is called a phoenix. It has bright red and gold feathers and is linked to the worship of the sun. Did you know that only one phoenix can exist at a time? It can live for 500 years or more. In Greek mythology, a phoenix reborn from the flames is said to be even more spectacular than before.

DIFFICULTY: EASY   **TIME:** 1 HOUR

PHOENIX

Let's kick things off with this phoenix build. It's a fun and easy one to start with, and it will give you a chance to warm up before taking on the more challenging builds!

MATERIALS

Your final build will rise high from the ashes and fly high!

STEP 1

For this build, it's best to start with the torso. Use red blocks to make a frame, as shown. The biggest part of the body should be the middle section, going down at each end to form a tail and neck. Then you can begin filling it in.

STEP 2

Use this picture as a guide for how to create the neck. Build four rows of blocks out, away from the front of the torso. This will make a good base for adding the head and face.

STEP 3

Add more red blocks around the tip of the neck. We've outlined the blocks that you finished with in step 2 to help you figure out where they go!

End of neck from step 2

STEP 4

Grab some yellow and black blocks for eyes – these go in the gaps, like this! Then use more red blocks to give your beast its cheeks and a nose.

STEP 5

Give your phoenix its beak by building around the front of the face with yellow blocks. Use the image on the far right to build the bottom section of the open beak.

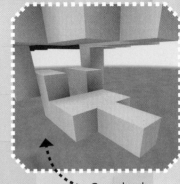

····· Open beak

STEP 6

A mix of yellow and orange blocks make great head feathers when they're built in rows, like this.

STEP 7

For the wing frame, create a shape each side of the monster's body. This is what it should look like from above.

STEP 8

Add a row of orange blocks, following the inside of the wing shape that you created in step 7. Repeat this with yellow blocks next and then try forming points, as shown below. Next, add a row of yellow blocks all the way down its back.

STEP 9

Build a fork-shaped tail coming off the back of its body using yellow blocks. The middle strip should be shorter.

STEP 10

Complete the tail by adding a row of orange blocks to the outside of the frame. Then add a few red blocks, like this!

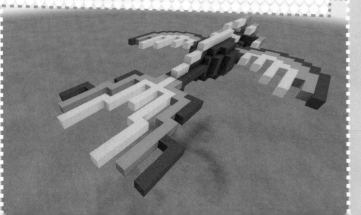

STEP 11

Add two yellow legs underneath the body. The feet should be bending backwards to show that your phoenix is flying. Finally, add brown claws and you're all done!

DIFFICULTY: INTERMEDIATE   **TIME:** 2 HOURS

GRIFFIN

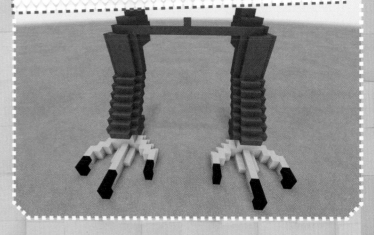

This legendary creature has the body of a lion and the wings and head of an eagle. Basically, they're awesome. Just follow the steps to create your own!

MATERIALS

The **griffin** is also known as **griffon** or **gryphon**.

STEP 1

Begin by building a three-clawed foot using yellow blocks. Then start to layer up the foot with more blocks. Add black blocks to the tips of the claws, like this.

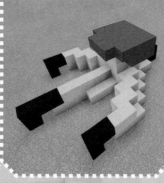

STEP 3

When you've built about seven rows of stepped blocks, add the straight sections of the legs. Now it's time to join up the legs. Do this by building a bar of brown blocks from one leg to the other, like this.

STEP 2

Next use brown blocks to form the griffin's ankle, and then its leg. To create a bend in the leg, build the blocks so that they slope backwards. Repeat steps 1 and 2 to make the second foot and leg.

STEP 4

Make a loop of brown blocks to form a frame for the creature's back. Keep adding to the frame until it looks 3D, just like the pictures on the right. This will make it easier to get a shape that you're happy with!

STEP 5

Now it's time to flesh out your griffin by filling in the frame. Keep adding the blocks to fill in its back.

This is what your monster should look like as you fill in the frame with plenty of blocks.

STEP 6

Fill out the torso by building across in layers, like this. The chest should reach down pretty close to the ground. Use white blocks at the top to begin shaping the neck!

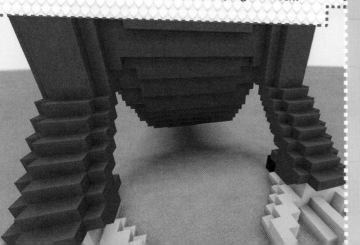

These images show you how to add your back legs. Start by building a circle of brown blocks on the back of the torso, then fill this in. Add some feet with black claws, then repeat this step to make the second back leg.

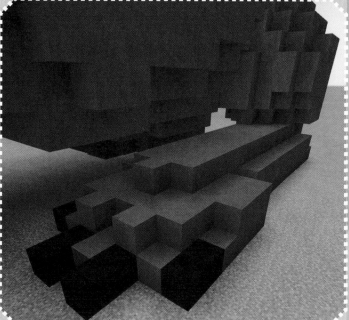

STEP 8

Make a head frame coming from the top of the neck that you started in step 6. Once you're happy with the shape, begin filling in the frame with lots of white blocks until it's solid.

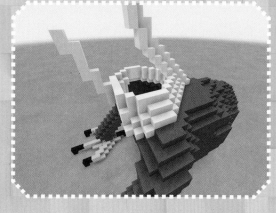

STEP 9

Give your griffin a big yellow beak coming out from the centre of its face, like this. Then use yellow and black blocks for an eye on each side.

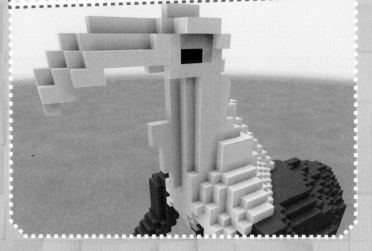

STEP 10

Create a curved tail shape coming from the back of your griffin. Fill it in with brown blocks, then add a cluster of black blocks to form the tip of the tail – it should look pointed.

STEP 11

For the griffin's wings, make them connect at the base of its white neck. Then create a strip of more white blocks to help you get the right shape for the wingspan. Play around with the shape until you're happy, then fill it in.

STEP 12

Now you've completed your build, zoom out to take a look at your monster. This is a good time for you to decide whether you want to make any final tweaks or adjustments.

Our **griffin** is looking totally magnificent. No doubt yours is too!

DIFFICULTY: MASTER   **TIME:** 3+ HOURS

MANTICORE

Are you ready to take on the magnificent manticore build? Word has it that these beasts could devour three humans in one go, without leaving so much as a trace!

MATERIALS

The manticore's teeth were meant to be shark-like.

+ STEP 1

For the two front feet, grab yourself some dark yellow blocks. Start by building a flat shape (one block high) as shown in the image below. Repeat this for the second one!

+ STEP 2

When you're happy with its feet, build up to create a leg shape that bends like this.

STEP 3

Now it's time to connect up the legs! Simply build a straight band of yellow blocks across, as shown. This will be the basis for forming the manticore's torso in step 4.

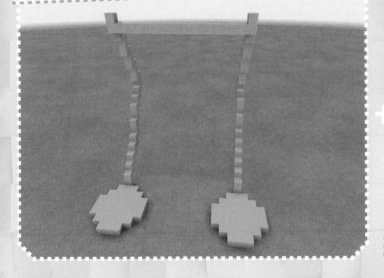

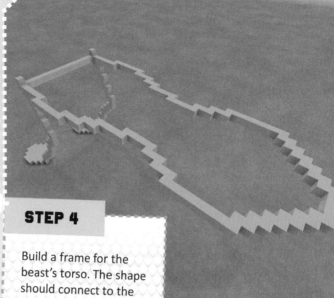

STEP 4

Build a frame for the beast's torso. The shape should connect to the top of the legs and look something like this.

STEP 5

To make your manticore look super-duper, it needs a 3D body. Add to the frame by building a curved underbelly that reaches from the front to the back of its torso.

STEP 6

Continue filling out the rest of frame. Start adding curved bands of blocks in a 'U' shape, that reach from left to right. This will create a more realistic and rounded body shape.

'U' shape bands help form torso!

STEP 7

Use this image as a guide for designing the back legs. The two back legs should be wide at the top, getting narrower at the bottom so that they're only a couple of blocks wide.

You're bound to get a kick out of this part of your beastly build!

STEP 8

Stay at the back of the body and start filling in the gaps to make it a solid structure. It works best to build in layers.

back

STEP 9

This is where your beast really starts to take shape. Keep filling in the rest of its body using layers of yellow blocks. Each layer should be narrower than the one below it.

STEP 10

Don't forget to fill out the back legs. Once you've got a flat surface, you can build them up using two more layers of yellow blocks, as shown on the right. Have a go!

Each layer is slightly smaller than the one underneath it.

STEP 11

Watch out – the back of your monster still needs filling in. Use your blocks to give it a rounded shape just like we've done below. You can start filling in the underbelly, too!

Underbelly

STEP 12

Next, fill in its chest. As you work your way downwards, the blocks should get narrower to form an upside down triangle. Keep going until you join up with the underbelly you built.

STEP 13

Make sure that your build is a cut above the rest by adding contours to the sides of its torso. Adding these details will give your manticore a muscular look.

Play around with contours to make your monsters look extra professional!

STEP 14

The front legs are probably looking a bit spindly right now! Go on, fill them out using the images on the right as a handy guide. Remember that you can try out your own techniques as these are just suggestions!

STEP 15

Finally it's your chance to mix things up with some black blocks. Add some to the back of your builld, like this. Then keep building them out to form its terrifying tail.

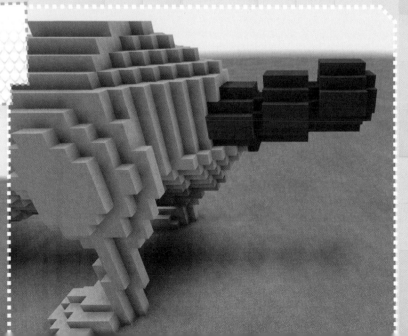

STEP 16

This is the fun bit! Let's give the manticore tail a stinger. There is quite a lot of detail in one of these so why not follow the illustrated steps labelled A to D to help you?

A

B

C

D

STEP 17

Now that the back of the monster is looking finished, move back to the **mane** event – get it?! Yes, this manticore is in serious need of a mane. With brown blocks, build a ring around the top of its shoulders.

STEP 18

Now map out the shape and size of its mane and head by creating a frame. Remember to leave a round face shape.

STEP 19

Use brown blocks to completely fill in the mane. Try your best to keep the overall shape as rounded as you can! It should now look a bit like this.

Space for the face!

STEP 20

It's back to the yellow blocks for the face! This is where things get more detailed. Give your monster a face, leaving space for the two eyes. Then create a snout. Look carefully at the picture below for how to form the ideal shape using your yellow blocks.

STEP 21

Wake up your manticore (we dare you!) by adding white and black blocks for its big beady eyes. Then, add a shiny black nose. Looking fierce!

STEP 22

Open wide! Use a few yellow blocks to form the creature's bottom jaw. Just be sure to leave it open wide enough for some large teeth.

STEP 23

Say 'ahhh!' Add a simple purple tongue inside your monster's mouth. WARNING! Only do this BEFORE step 24 or you risk being manticore grub! Just saying...

STEP 24

Finish the mouth by adding some pearly whites. We've given ours two large fangs. Looks pretty awesome, right?

STEP 25

Last but not least, we have the wings. First, build a simple black frame coming from the top of each shoulder. Then, all you need to do is fill them in using white blocks. Simple yet effective!

STEP 26

Take a moment to admire your marvellous manticore. Now you have the chance to go back and add more details to certain areas, if you fancy. We recommend adding more blocks to thicken its legs. Have fun experimenting and see how you get on!

NORSE
« MONSTERS »

This section is dedicated to a gruesome group that make up the Norse monsters. Not sure what they are? You'll be surprised how many of them crop up in your fave movies and TV shows. Think giants, dragons, serpents and elves. Here is our pick of the bunch!

« TROLL »

We know about the toys and the 2016 movie, but the original troll dates way back! It appears in Scandinavian folklore as a creature who lives in castles and haunts the area at night.

« WORLD SERPENT »

This slippery serpent of the sea is sometimes known as the Jörmungandr, which means 'huge monster' in Old Norse. The story goes that the World Serpent grew so big that its body wrapped right around the world and touched its own tail, and that's how it got its name.

We would NOT want to cross paths with this club-swinging **troll**.

SLEIPNIR

Sleipnir is a magical eight-legged horse ridden by the warrior god, Odin. Its eight legs are thought to represent the compass, as well as its ability to travel through the air or on land. With his large and muscular physique, Sleipnir is known to be powerful and fearless.

KRAKEN

Is the kraken the biggest monster ever? The multi-legged sea creature is from Scandinavian folklore and haunts the seas along the coast of Norway and Greenland. They wrap their legs around ships to sink them, or create whirlpools to drag them under!

FENRIR WOLF

This monstrous creature is the Fenrir. He's son of the god, Loki, and the giantess, Angerboda. Fenrir would skulk about waiting for a chance to gobble up any gods that he could. So the gods made a chain to control Fenrir (very wise!) using a mix of mythical ingredients, such as a fish's breath and a woman's beard.

Haunting the seas, the giant **Kraken** drags ships down under the water or creates a whirlpool to do it.

FENRIR WOLF

This wild wolf is all about death and destruction, so keep your wits about you as you build.

MATERIALS

We've created a **Fenrir wolf** that's lying down and ready to pounce!

STEP 1

For this beastly build, start with the legs. Make a rectangular leg shape using grey blocks. Add some blocks to look like claws, as shown.

STEP 2

Build upwards (about four to five blocks high) for the upper leg. Repeat these steps to make another leg in line with the first. Don't make them too close together!

STEP 3

To connect your two legs, create a circle using more grey blocks. This will form the basic frame for its hips and torso. Top tip – the bottom of the circle should be super close to the ground, but not quite touching it.

STEP 4

For the body, build a loop of blocks coming off the top of the circle you made in step 3. It should join back up to the bottom of the circle. Start filling it in, as shown on the right.

STEP 5

It's time to give it a fierce face! Look at the image to the right to help you get the shape just right. Be sure to give it a long, pointy snout. Next we'll bring the face to life with the all-important details.

STEP 6

For the pointed ears, add black blocks with a couple of pale grey ones inside each. Pop in a set of creepy green eyes, framed with black blocks to make them stand out!

STEP 7

Two white blocks are all you need to create these nasty gnashers!

You can use pale grey blocks for its fluffy underbelly, like this.

STEP 8

Your wolf is missing its back legs! Build a stump on each side of the back of its torso (bottom left), with grey blocks. Then repeat steps 1 and 2 to complete the legs and feet.

STEP 9

All the best monsters have tails, right? Get hold of some pale grey blocks and make a cross shape on the end of its body. Keep adding to the tail until it's wiggly and long.

DIFFICULTY: INTERMEDIATE   **TIME: 2 HOURS**

KRAKEN

You're unlikely to come across a sea monster that's more leg-tastic than a kraken. Make sure that your creation is as fabulous as the real deal. You can do it!

MATERIALS

STEP 1

Start by creating a head frame for your kraken with some orange blocks. Create a circle flat on the ground, then add a loop to make your monster 3D. Continue adding bands of orange blocks to form the shape of its head.

Why not experiment with giving your **kraken** a pool of water to splash around in?

STEP 2

Now it's time to fill in the kraken's head with more orange blocks, like this.

STEP 3

Use purple blocks for its large eyes. For the nose, add more orange blocks between the eyes. Use this picture to help you to get the face shape just right!

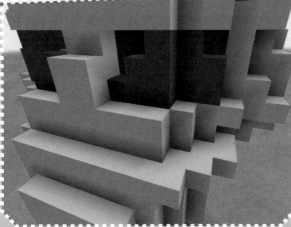

You can add or take away blocks to experiment with your **kraken's** face.

STEP 4

Red blocks at the ready for the brow! The red eyebrow should follow the shape of the eyes and nose, like this.

Build the walls of a pool big enough for your **kraken** to sit in, then fill with water using your water bucket.

STEP 5

Use light purple flat blocks to make a bottom eyelid, as shown. This makes the eyes really pop!

STEP 6

Create a simple leg frame, as shown in the image below. They should join the body underneath the kraken's head. It works well if the legs are not too straight! Have a go...

STEP 7

When you're happy with the shape of its leg frame, you can fill it in completely.

STEP 8

Try to keep a hollow groove running along the underside of the kraken's leg. In the next step, you will use a different colour to fill this section in!

Hollow groove

STEP 9

Now it's time to fill in the hollow groove (from step 8) with purple blocks. This extra detail will really set your monster build apart from the rest!

STEP 10

For the icing on the cake, you can add suckers! All you need to do is drop on some white cubes to the underside of the tentacle.

STEP 11

Now that you've created one tentacle, you'll need to repeat these steps until you have eight. Once that's done, your build is complete! How about adding some blue blocks for water?

STEP 12

Now build up four walls around your kraken – make sure there are no gaps! Now fill this up with your water bucket.

DIFFICULTY: MASTER   **TIME:** 3+ HOURS

THE
WORLD SERPENT

Master this fierce-faced monster and you are bound to impress your Minecraft mates!

MATERIALS

STEP 1

Before adding any detail, we need to start with the shape of the serpent's body. Use this picture as a guide.

The body of the World Serpent should be coiled around, with its head raised off the ground.

The head should be up away from the ground.

STEP 2

Starting with the tip, give your monster a bright blue tail, like this.

STEP 3

To create a base for its body you'll need your pale yellow blocks. Build wall-like structures to create a groove running all the way along your serpent's body.

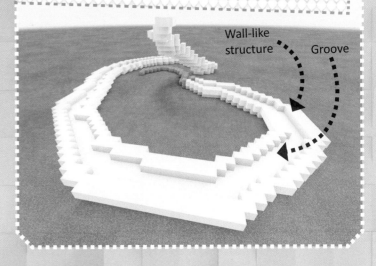

Wall-like structure   Groove

STEP 4

Next you'll be adding blue arches right the way along the length of the body. They should join from one side of the wall to the other, as shown.

STEP 5

Use your blue blocks to fill in the spaces between the arches that you built in step 4. You should now have a hollow snake torso.

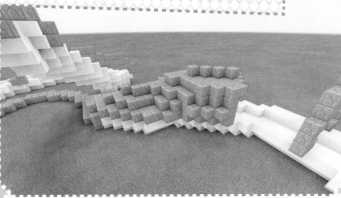

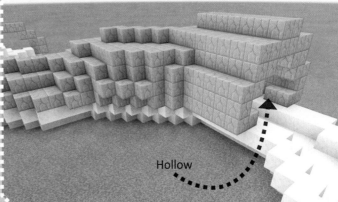

Hollow

STEP 6

Continue filling in the body. Experiment with layering blocks to make a shape that's as rounded as possible.

STEP 7

Once the entire body is filled in, you can start to fill in the neck. The neck should be narrower than the main part of the body.

STEP 8

Use blue blocks to form the shape of the World Serpent's head. This image gives you an idea of how many blocks to use.

The neck steps down from the head to the coiled body.

STEP 9

Next, start to fill in the face details. The front of the face should be narrower. Leave a space for an eye on each side of its head. Look at these images for inspiration!

STEP 10

The top of its head should now look something like this!

STEP 11

Get underneath the monster to form its bottom jaw shape. This comes out as far as the upper jaw.

Is it just us, or is that mouth just waiting to be packed with fangs?

STEP 12

You've got the bottom jaw shape so now you can fill it in. Look at how the blocks come down like steps from the back of its mouth.

Inside its mouth

STEP 13

Use pink blocks to create gums ready for its fangs. These blocks can be added to the roof of its mouth and to create a tongue on the bottom, too!

STEP 14

Those gums need some fangs! Add white blocks and dot them around the upper and lower jawline, as shown.

STEP 15

Right now, you can probably see straight through its empty eye socket! Fix this pronto by adding one black block with a yellow block each side of it. Repeat this on the other side.

We love the winding body raising its head out to meet us.

If you like, you can go back to add more blocks. This can be a good time to perfect the shape of your build.

GREEK
《 MYTHS 》

Stories of gods and monsters were an important part of Ancient Greek culture. These tales helped them to understand everything from life and death to the weather! Greek mythology is where minotaurs, cyclops and centaurs come to life. Take a look at these fascinating mythological creatures and see how many you recognise!

《 PEGASUS 》

You may not know that monstrous snake-haired Medusa was Pegasus' mother. For real! The story goes that Pegasus was created from the blood that was shed when Perseus beheaded Medusa. This immortal, flying horse has large and impressive wings. There is even a constellation named after Pegasus. Pretty cool, right?

The elegant **Pegasus** is the son of Poseidon and the Gorgon, Medusa.

CYCLOPS

This super strong, one-eyed giant is a cyclops. According to legend, the cyclops were a group of rule-breaking shepherds who ate humans. This monstrous being was not even afraid of the gods – which is either brave or stupid! Its singular eye doesn't just look awesome, but it also fires out energy beams.

Cyclops means 'round eyed'. The eye is in the centre of his forehead.

MINOTAUR

As you can see, the monstrous Minotaur of Crete is a bull crossed with a human. It's one of the most well-known beasts in Greek mythology. The minotaur was kept hidden in the middle of a complex labyrinth so that it couldn't escape! While in its dark labyrinth home, it was fed a diet of young humans.

Minotaurs have the body of a man and a bull's head and tail.

CENTAUR

Check out the centaur! This mythological being lives in the forests and mountains of Greece. It is easy to recognize with its human head and torso, on top of a horse's lower body. Centaurs are pretty smart and they are able to speak.

CERBERUS

This multi-headed dog is sometimes called the 'hound of Hades' because it guards the gates of the Underworld. The ferocious Cerberus would devour the dead when they tried to escape back to the land of the living. Cerberus' monster parents were Echidna and Typhon.

Cerberus is sometimes described as having more than three heads.

DIFFICULTY: EASY   **TIME:** 1 HOUR

CYCLOPS

These bulging-eyed beasts are creepy creatures who appear in both Greek and Roman mythology. Are you ready to build your own? Let's do this...

STEP 1

Kick start this build with a leg. We've given ours a brown boot and a straight pale pink leg.

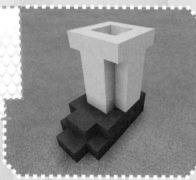

This **cyclops** looks awesome with a beard. Do you agree?

MATERIALS

STEP 2

Build the second leg so that it's a few blocks apart from the first one. Then, find some red blocks to make shorts. Use darker blocks for a waistband.

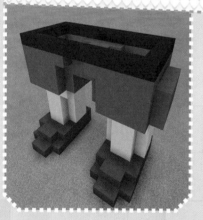

STEP 3

Give your cyclops a shirt using any colour blocks you like. Add a layer of blocks to the front to give him a more rounded and realistic look.

STEP 4

To build up the shoulders, start by creating these strap-like shapes to the top of the shirt, as shown. The top of these will become the top of its shoulders.

STEP 5

Now add pale pink blocks to give the cyclops shoulders. Be sure to make them mega muscly!

STEP 6

Keep adding pale pink blocks to give your cyclops arms. Now your build is really beginning to take shape!

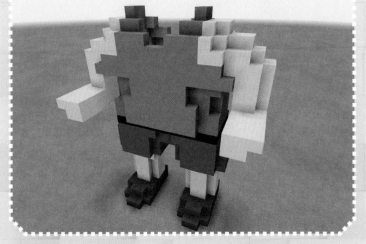

STEP 7

It's beard building time! It should sit between the shoulders. We used black, but you can choose any colour.

STEP 8

Build the face on top of the beard using pale pink blocks. Now give your cyclops a big eye using white, blue and one black block. Add a row of black blocks above the eye as a monobrow, completing its face with a pink nose.

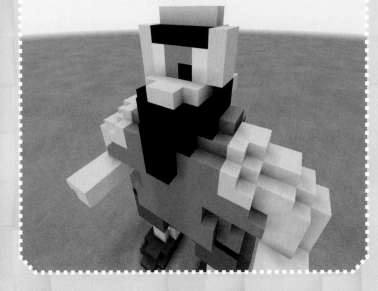

STEP 9

Make bent arms coming down from the shoulders. Use one block to give his right hand a thumb, like this.

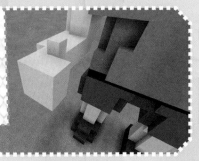

STEP 10

Use dark yellow blocks to make a club. Look below for how to get the shape right! The left hand should be slightly open so that the fingers can wrap around the club.

GREEK MYTHS

MINOTAUR

Up next is the maze-dwelling Minotaur. Check out that mighty axe! Choose your bricks and build.

MATERIALS

STEP 1

Make hooves with black blocks. Single rows of blocks make great toes! The hooves should be at least two blocks apart.

STEP 2

Next, create the legs and hips using brown blocks. Look at this image to help you make the knees bend slightly.

STEP 3

Add a layer of brown blocks to fill out the hips. This will be the base for your torso, so try making it oval shaped if you can.

Our **Minotaur** has a space of three blocks between its hooves. This helps keep your build balanced.

STEP 4

To build the bottom of its torso, use a darker brown block. This section should be roughly five blocks high. The fifth layer should be the widest part, as shown in the picture.

STEP 5

Time to give your monster its muscles! Add another layer of dark brown blocks to begin forming the Minotaur's chest. Use this picture as a guide for the pattern that your brown blocks should make.

STEP 6

Next, build out the frame for its back using the lighter brown blocks. Now you can start filling it in to form the torso. Your monster should now look a bit like this from the side.

STEP 7

Continue filling in the torso until it is solid. Then begin narrowing the shape as you work your way up. This will form the shoulders and neck. Copy the shoulder shape in the image on the right.

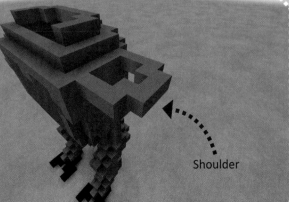

Shoulder

STEP 8

To build the big, strong arms, use lighter brown blocks. Build down from the shoulder that you created in step 7 until you reach the narrow part of its torso. Now repeat this for the other arm.

STEP 9

Build its forearms by creating a right angle with the blocks. The arms should reach forwards, like this.

STEP 10

Use the pictures on the right as a guide for building the hands. Be sure to leave enough space in the hands for them to hold the axe handle (see step 11).

STEP 11

Use yellow blocks to make a long, straight axe handle. The Minotaur's hands should be able to hold the axe handle flat, as seen below.

STEP 12

Now it is time to make the weapon look fierce! So, use grey blocks to create a whopping axe head. The top part should be slightly larger than the bottom bit.

STEP 13

Use brown blocks to build up the head. Look at the picture on the left as a guide.

STEP 14

Start building up the nose and snout area. Use black blocks for the nose holes.

STEP 15

At the end of the snout, create two beady eyes. Try using yellow blocks to frame the black pupils.

STEP 16

Now build up the rest of face. The layers should get narrower as you work your way to the top of its head. Add some darker brown blocks as hair!

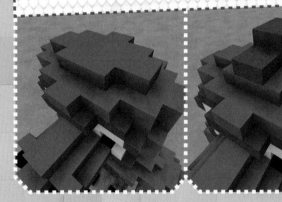

STEP 17

You could give your monster a jazzy nose ring. Try gold blocks for extra spangle!

STEP 18

Grey blocks make perfect horns on each side of its head. They should be pointed at the ends.

DIFFICULTY: MASTER   **TIME:** 3+ HOURS

CERBERUS

In the myth, this three-headed hound called Cerberus would hang out near the River Styx.

MATERIALS

Three heads are better than one!

STEP 1

First, build a three-toed front paw with grey blocks, like this. Repeat this for the next foot but make sure they're further apart than usual!

Three heads are better than one!

With this build, the torso needs to be wide enough to hold all three beastly heads.

STEP 2

For the legs, add a row of grey blocks slanting back. Then add a disc shape to the end. This is where it will connect up to Cerberus' body. Do the same for the second leg.

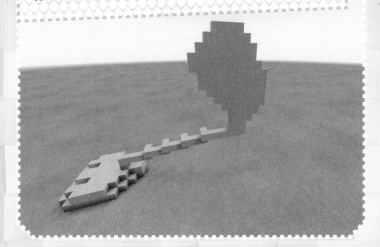

STEP 3

Use a line of grey blocks to join up the two front legs. This row of blocks should attach to the insides of the grey discs.

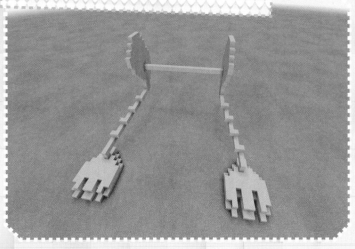

STEP 4

Create a quick frame for the basic body shape. This will help you to decide on the size and shape before you get carried away with filling it all in or adding details.

STEP 5

Add a line for its underbelly which reaches from the back to the front of the body. You can then build the upper leg outline, like this!

Upper leg outline.

STEP 6

Next, join up the creature's shoulders by building a row of grey blocks from the top of the grey discs that you made back in step 2.

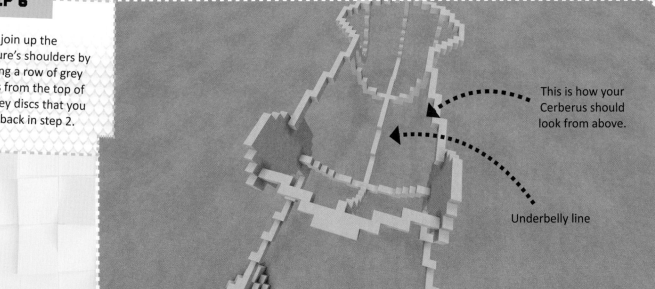

This is how your Cerberus should look from above.

Underbelly line

STEP 7

Grab grey blocks to fill in the bottom layer of your build. The underbelly should be quite close to the ground. Look at the steps ahead to give you a better idea!

STEP 8

Fill out the whole underbelly until there are no spaces left, all the way to the middle of the torso.

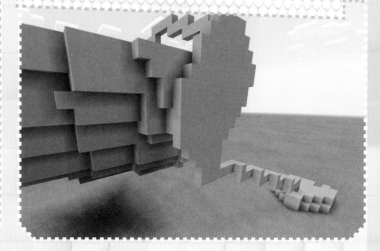

STEP 9

Build a frame for the top of the torso by adding bands of grey blocks arching over from one side to the other. This will look a bit like a tunnel!

STEP 10

Next fill in the top of the torso until it looks like this. Layer up the blocks to create contours. If it doesn't work first time, just take them away and try again!

STEP 11

At the front of your monster, add some dark grey chest fur. You can follow the basic pattern in the image below, or have a go at your own!

STEP 12

Give it some muscle! Build up the front legs with more grey blocks to make it look mega powerful. Look at the picture to see how to make the ankles.

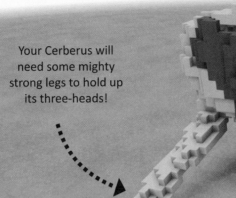

Your Cerberus will need some mighty strong legs to hold up its three-heads!

STEP 13

Find some black blocks to add some claw details to its feet. If you don't like the colour scheme, make up your own!

All the best monster builds have clawsome details like this!

STEP 14

Complete the back legs, build a frame that comes off the hips and reaches down to the ground. The picture on the right should give you an idea of how big each back leg must be!

STEP 15

You've nailed the shape, so now it's time to fill in the back legs. Don't build all the way to the ground for now. We'll tell you why in step 16.

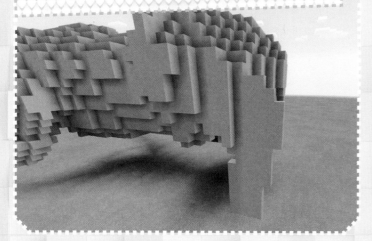

STEP 16

Just before the legs reach the ground, build a little stump on the end of each foot. The stumps need to be facing forwards as this is what you will use to build the feet.

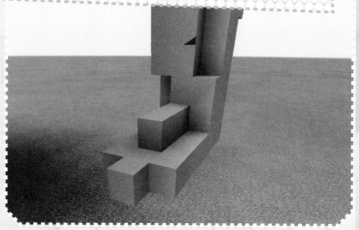

STEP 17

Build a foot on the end of one of the stumps that you've just built and give it three toes. Repeat these steps to make the other foot match.

STEP 18

Pop on some claws on each toe with black blocks. The contrasting colours are super-effective at making them really pop!

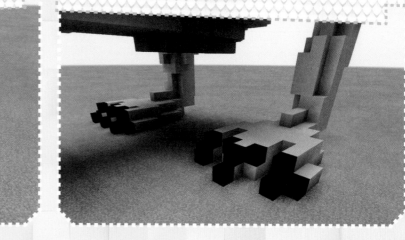

STEP 19

Begin to form the three necks and heads. Keep these outlines as simple as possible, until you know that you can fit all three. Otherwise it'll be a big waste of time! Details come later, friends!

Add a little tail

STEP 20

The next stage is to create a flat surface on each of the heads, as shown. Eventually, this will form the upper jaw and the base for its oodles of beady eyes!

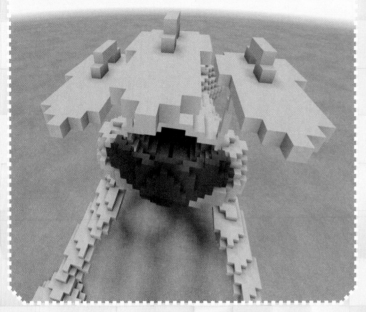

STEP 21

Underneath each head, try building a wall all the way around the edges. This will form the creature's gums.

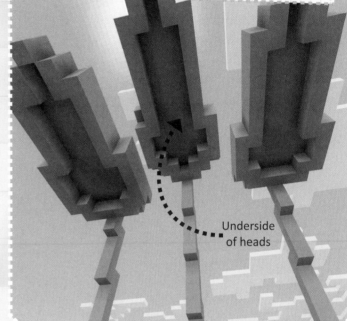

Underside of heads

STEP 22

Here's how to build the lower jaw. Pick one head and create steps down underneath the back of the head. The more steps, the more open the mouth will be. Now fill it in.

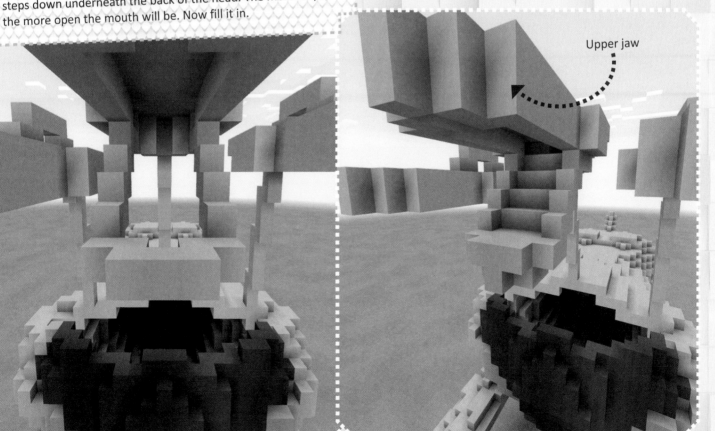

Upper jaw

STEP 23

Next make the top of the head by adding an extra layer of grey blocks to the upper jaw. For the snout, mark out a 'T' shape, like this.

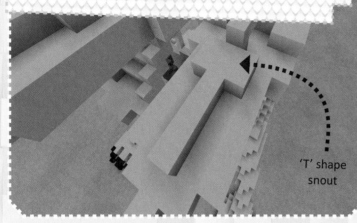

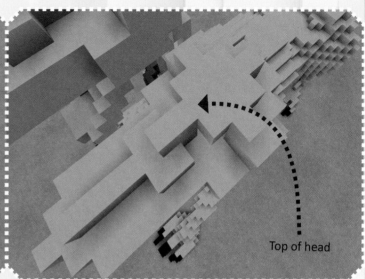

'T' shape snout

Top of head

STEP 24

Repeat steps 22 and 23 for the other two heads. You can play around with how open or closed the jaws are on each head, like we have done!

STEP 25

Take the scary levels up a notch with some glowing red eyeballs! We reckon they look awesome – what do you think? Frame all six eyes with dark grey eyebrows.

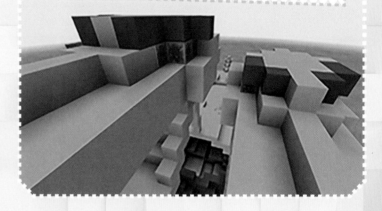

STEP 26

Keep hold of the dark grey blocks to build the ears! Make them simple though as you need to create them six times! Now use black blocks for their cube-shaped noses. Wow!

STEP 27

Add a layer of pink blocks to the insides of their mouths. Then drop in plenty of white teeth. ROOOAR!

STEP 28

Their necks are looking a bit thin so it's time to flesh them out. Begin by adding another row of grey blocks to each neck, from the shoulders to where it joins the head.

STEP 29

Now all that is left to do is fill in the neck frames so that they are good and solid. And your Cerberus is done!

In this pose, your **Cerberus** looks ready to pounce on unsuspecting victims.

AROUND THE

《 # WORLD 》

It's time to take a quick break from building. So put down your tools and explore the planet's most famous mythological creatures. How brave are you feeling? Because you're about to discover the monstrous stories, folkores and fairy tales that brought us the yeti, the sphinx, the vampire, and MORE! Let's do this...

《 YETI 》

If you don't know what a yeti is, imagine a big hairy creature that looks a bit like an ape. Yeti actually means 'wild man' in Sherpa. Sometimes known as the Abominable Snowman, the yeti calls the Himalayan region of India, Nepal and China home. It is so strong that people believe the yeti can kill with just one punch.

The **yeti** is described as much taller than humans.

《 KAPPA 》

The kappa is a scaly, turtle-like humanoid found in Japanese folklore. It lives in rivers and ponds and is much less nimble on land. The top of its head is shaped to carry water, which is its power source – it can't move if this is empty!

VAMPIRE

We've all heard of Dracula, right? No doubt he's the most famous fanged, blood-guzzling vampire ever. Vampires prey on live humans and feast on their blood. Want to know something really creepy? A vampire can't see their reflection in a mirror. Word has it that you can get rid of a vampire with garlic! Worth a try.

CHUPACABRA

Legend has it that the chupacabra loves nothing more than slurping on the blood of livestock. The first sighting of this beastly creature was in Puerto Rico. It's tricky to know what it looks like as the descriptions range from reptile-like to a hairless dog. One thing is for sure – it has a whopping set of fangs and claws to boot!

SPHINX

The sphinx crops up in Greek and Egyptian mythology. With the body of a lion and the head of a human, the sphinx is a unique creature. Sometimes shown with large eagle wings, in Ancient Egypt, the sphinx's head was often made to look like a pharaoh or god.

LOCH NESS

Fresh from the Scottish Highlands, the Loch Ness Monster, or Nessie, is a whopping, long-necked beast that lives in the water. The first sighting was in 1933 by George Spicer from London. Images often show it with humps poking out of the water.

DIFFICULTY: EASY   **TIME:** 1 HOUR

KAPPA

Your next build challenge comes in the form of a kappa. This version of the mysterious, turtle-like river monster is cute, but watch out - it's still pretty dangerous!

MATERIALS

STEP 1

Make two green feet with three toes on each. Build up the legs, like this.

The **kappa** has a hollow disc-like shape on top of its head for carrying water.

STEP 2

Create the bottom of the torso in yellow. Aim for an upside down triangle shape, like this.

STEP 3

Add more yellow blocks to form its stomach. Use some green blocks as shoulders, like this.

STEP 4

From the shoulders, build two green arms. Give each hand three fingers.

STEP 5

Check out the picture on the right to see how your kappa should look from behind. To create its shell, begin with a simple frame that reaches up to the shoulders and down to the top of its legs.

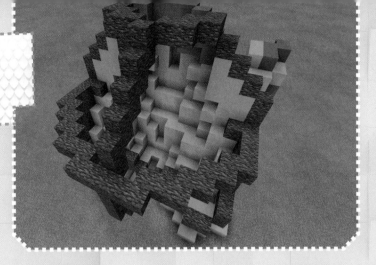

STEP 6

Continue filling in the shell until it is solid with no gaps. The kappa should have a curved shape, like this.

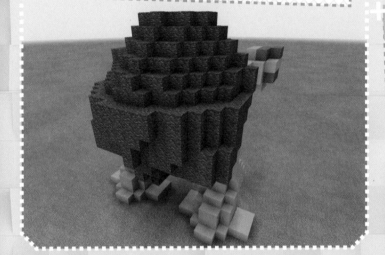

STEP 7

Create a frame using green blocks for the front of its head and leave eye gaps. Then make a yellow beak.

STEP 8

Bright orange blocks are great for evil eyes! Pop two black blocks in for pupils.

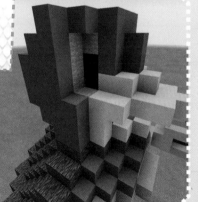

STEP 9

To make your kappa look just like the real deal, use black blocks as hair. Then use brown blocks in a disc shape on top of the hair, like this.

STEP 10

Finally, stick one grey block to the tip of each finger to look like claws. Do the same for the feet and your build will look completely ferocious in no time! You're finished.

YETI

Now you get to create your very own yeti, fresh from the Himalayan mountains.

This build shouldn't be abominably tricky – just follow these simple steps!

STEP 1

To build your yeti, start with its foot. Look at the picture below to help you get the shape right. Then, use purple blocks to give it claws.

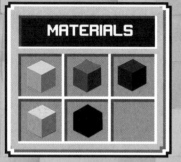

STEP 2

Start building the leg frame coming out from the base of the foot. Try building it in steps so that the knee is bending forwards.

STEP 3

Fill in the leg with lots of grey blocks. Then, build across to form the hips. Check out the picture below and use it as a guide for how many blocks to use!

STEP 4

When the hips are wide enough, you can add the second leg. Then repeat steps 1 and 2 to add a second foot and claws, too!

STEP 5

The below image shows how your monster should look from behind. Layer up some more grey blocks to make its bottom.

STEP 6

Get hold of some purple blocks to build the stomach. Add these blocks to the front of the monster's hips. Make the edges of the stomach look like fur by leaving spaces between the blocks, as shown.

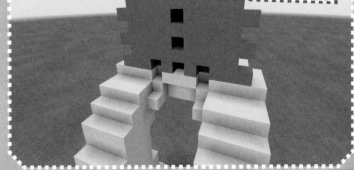

STEP 7

Make its chest muscles by adding panels of purple blocks near the top of the yeti's stomach. The panels should be peaked at the top, as shown.

STEP 8

With your grey blocks, build a border right the way around the chest muscles that you've made in step 7. There must be no gaps and it should look like the below!

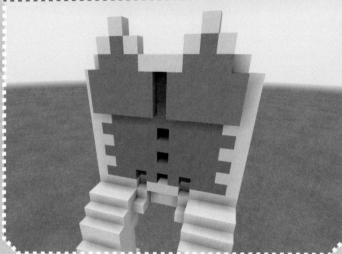

STEP 9

Keep building up the grey blocks. Don't forget to work your way around to the back of the yeti. It should be hollow, like this.

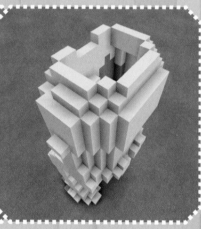

STEP 10

For the yeti's face, begin by using purple blocks. Leave large gaps for the eyes and mouth so that it looks a little like a mask! Make an upside down 'T' for the nose.

STEP 11

Add a row of grey blocks to border the face that you've built. Then fill in the back and sides of its head with more grey blocks. It's as easy as that!

STEP 12

Use around three layers of grey blocks to form the top of its head. Then give the eyebrows extra definition with an extra row of grey blocks over each eye.

STEP 13

The top of the arms should be in-line with the top of the purple chest. Use grey blocks to build down in steps. We made each arm four blocks wide at the top.

STEP 14

Create an elbow halfway down the arm so that the forearm can reach forwards. Now repeat these steps for the other arm and try to make them match, if you can!

STEP 15

Add purple blocks to give the yeti its thumbs and fingers on both hands. This will help to give the hands definition!

STEP 16

Finish off the yeti's frightening face by filling in the mouth with a darker shade of purple blocks. Finally, use pale yellow for the eyes, along with a black block for the pupils.

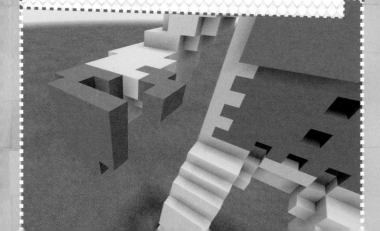

DIFFICULTY: MASTER   **TIME:** 3+ HOURS

SPHINX

Statues of sphinxes are often found guarding tombs and temples, but now it's your turn to create your own. Ready, set, build!

MATERIALS

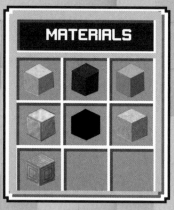

STEP 1

Like with lots of the builds in this book, we're starting with a foot frame. Follow the shape in the picture as a guide for placing your blocks.

STEP 2

Fill in the frame with the same colour. We have added three layers to the foot. Build up in steps from the claws.

Today the **sphinx** represents wisdom and strength.

The iconic **sphinx** pose is instantly recognisable!

STEP 3

Build the leg so that it is lying flat along the ground.
Look at the pictures to help you with the shape.

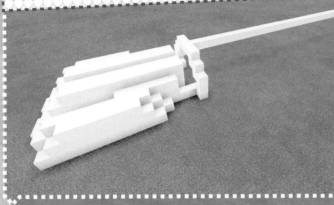

STEP 4

Start to build a simple frame for the front
of the torso and the second leg.

STEP 5

Build the second leg and the foot. Look back at
the previous steps to help you, or copy the first
one you built!

STEP 6

Continue building the torso frame so that it looks like the picture below. The back section should have a smooth curve!

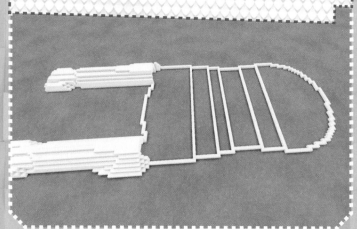

STEP 7

Build up the frame for the sphinx's back. Try copying what we've done below, or experiment with your own technique!

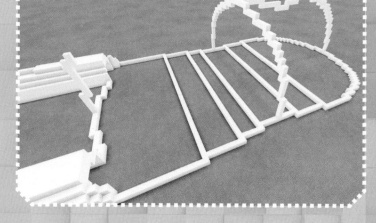

STEP 8

Work your way down the sphinx's body, building frames for the shoulders and neck. It looks trickier than it really is, honestly!

Frames for the shoulders.

STEP 9

You've mapped out and planned its body, so now it's time to fill it all in. As always, create curved shapes using plenty of layers of blocks in steps.

STEP 10

Begin creating a frame for its head. The bottom of the head should sit just above the shoulder frame!

STEP 11

Extend the frame out behind. Here you can create the curve of the back of its head.

Curved back of head

STEP 12

Below is the side view of the front leg. Fill in the shoulders on both sides so they are solid shapes.

Front legs

Shoulders

STEP 13

Add plenty of blocks to fill in your sphinx's chest, like this.

Front legs

STEP 14

Create the shape of its back leg. It should be laid flat along the ground and the feet should reach about halfway down the torso.

STEP 15

Begin filling in its back leg. Bulk up the leg join by layering lots of blocks up. Now repeat this on the other side.

Look at the image on the right for how to create the outline of a headdress with stone colour blocks. Then add gold blocks to build a frame around the face. It wouldn't be a sphinx without glorious golden touches!

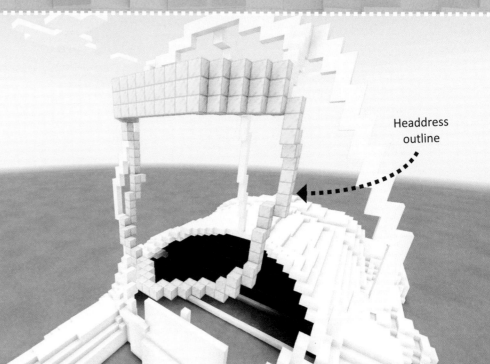

Headdress outline

Now build a golden beard shape at the bottom of the gold frame, as shown below. The beard should reach about halfway down its chest!

See below for how to add blue stripes to the sphinx's headdress. Build the stripes backwards to form the back of its rounded head.

STEP 19

Now fill in the gaps between the blue stripes with bands of gold blocks. Do this all the way down the headdress until all the gaps are filled in.

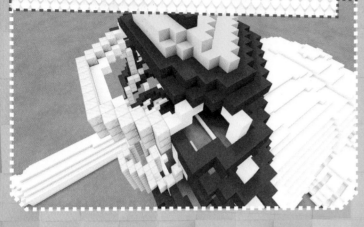

STEP 20

Hurrah – the finished headdress will look like this! Use your blocks to build a big cross over its hollow face.

STEP 21

Look at the picture for how to start filling in the face. First, build a nose shape where the big cross meets. The horizontal lines will become the cheekbones.

Cheeks

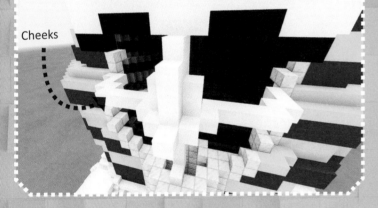

STEP 22

Keep filling in the face details so that you have a nose, mouth and cheeks. Give it some bold black eyebrows and leave two large holes for its eyes.

STEP 23

For the eyes, all you need is five white blocks. Lay four in a row, then add one directly below, like this!

STEP 24

Add a vibrant green cobra detail for the finishing touch. You have made your sphinx!

EPIC ≪SHOWDOWNS≫

We've heard all about the beastly monsters of myths and legends, but what about the heroes who courageously defeated them? Let's celebrate the heroes who faced these infamous monsters, from Bellerophon to Hercules and Beowulf! Who will be your fave?

≪ BELLEROPHON VS CHIMERA ≫

The greek hero, Bellerophon, is known for being a slayer of monsters. Chimera had been causing chaos, terrifying and murdering the people of Greece. So when Bellerophon defeated her it was massive news. According to the myth, Bellerophon shot and killed the fire-breathing monster from the sky, while flying on Pegasus. No wonder this made him legendary!

This is **Chimera** with her lion-like body, a goat's head on her back, and a slippery snake as a tail.

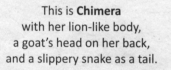

HERACLES VS NEMEAN LION

Heracles was the son of Zeus and Alcmene and a hero of Greek mythology (in Roman mythology he is known as Hercules). In the legend of the Labours of Heracles, King Eurytheus set Heracles the challenge of slaying the unstoppable Nemean lion which had skin that couldn't be penetrated by weapons. The beast did try to fight back and successfully chomped off one of his fingers – but that's about the only injury Heracles received. Unbelievably, Heracles managed to defeat the monster by strangling it with his bare hands. Now that's brave! He failed to skin the lion with his knife, but the goddess Athena suggested using the lion's own claw and this worked a treat!

The legend of the Labours of **Heracles** where **Heracles** slayed the monstrous **Nemean lion.**

BEOWULF VS GRENDEL

The story of Beowulf and Grendel is set in Scandinavia. The monstrous Grendel had been wreaking havoc at King Hrothgar's mead hall for 12 years. Every night, the beast would steal away and eat Hrothgar's warriors. Ghastly! This carried on until the daring Swedish prince Beowulf offered to rid them of the beast once and for all. The duo's fight resulted in Grendel losing an arm and being fatally wounded. The prince is then able to take the head from the dead Grendel and is hailed a hero.

The brave **Beowolf** defeated the deadly **Grendel** to become a hero.

DIFFICULTY: SUPREME MASTER   **TIME: 4+ HOURS**

CHIMERA

This monster has a goat's head coming out of its back.

Chimera has a snake as a tail. Yikes!

Chimeras are awesome and so is this step-by-step guide to making one in Minecraft!

STEP 1

Start with its two front feet. Layer up pale yellow blocks, as shown in the images below. This makes them look rounded. Don't forget to build four claws on each foot. Then begin to form the ankles.

MATERIALS

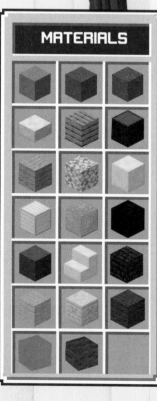

STEP 2

Build up from the ankles to make two legs, like this. Now create the back legs, but leave them as stumps.

These are the back feet. Keep them small for now.

STEP 3

The chimera has a set of hooves on its hind legs. You will need two shades of grey blocks to achieve this! Try pale grey for the ankles and dark grey for the hooves.

The hooves are split into two 'toes'.

STEP 4

Join up the four legs by creating a torso and neck. Use pale yellow blocks to create the below shape. When you're happy with it, use brown blocks to add shading – this will be the goat part. Use the picture on the right as a guide for where to add brown block detail to the back legs, too.

Neck

Back

STEP 5

It wouldn't be a chimera without its iconic mane! Start by adding a ring of dark brown blocks right the way around the neck that you built in step 4.

This bit is the **chimera's** neck area. The mane should frame the neck.

STEP 6

For the next part of the mane you'll need orange blocks.
Build a ring of them in front of the brown blocks. The
below image shows how the orange section should look!

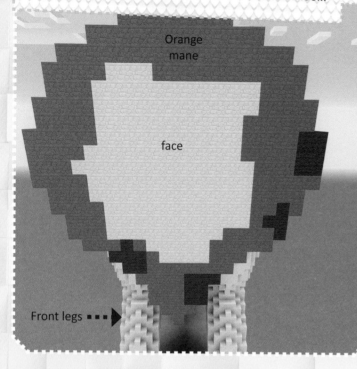

Orange
mane

face

Front legs ••••▶

This is a side view of your
monster. It shows you the
layers of brown and orange
blocks that make up the mane.

STEP 7

Now it's time to build up the lion face. Check out these
images to help you make the fierce face look super
realistic. At this stage, you should have around three
layers of blocks for the face section.

STEP 8

Let's fill in the face details! Map out the snout and eye area using more pale yellow blocks. It works best if you give the beast an open mouth! You'll be able to add in features using different coloured blocks in step 9 and 10.

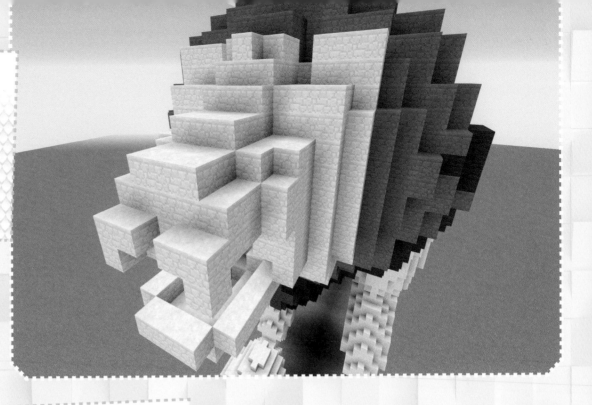

STEP 9

Brown blocks are best for the nose and pink is the obvious choice for its tongue. When these are complete, why not add some chompy white teeth? Roar!

STEP 10

Now add some white and black blocks for its two eyes. If you're not happy with the face, go back and play around with the blocks. Try adding more to get the shapes just right. Have fun experimenting!

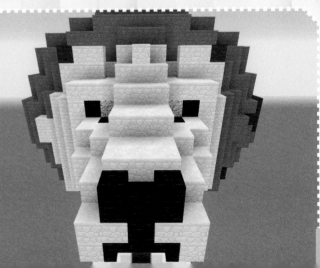

STEP 11

Add a shade of brown blocks along the spine of your chimera. This will give the creature some definition and it it will also form the base for the goat head.

Back of head

STEP 12

Use the same brown blocks for the goat neck. You should build the neck so that it joins about halfway down the monster's back.

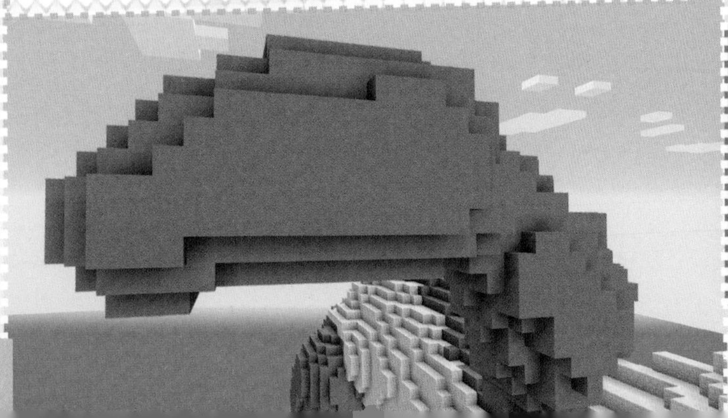

The goat head should taper down towards the nose area at the front of its face.

STEP 13

Next it's time to begin building the goat head, as shown below. Use the same brown blocks that you used for the neck!

STEP 14

Grab some black blocks and build a strip of them reaching from the head, all the way along the goat body. Then cover the head in a layer of black. This image shows you what it might look like from above.

View from above

STEP 15

Fill in some details underneath the neck of the goat that you've built. We reckon that grey blocks, like these, look best – but you can pick any colour!

STEP 16

This is where you can get really creative. Use pale blocks to build two curly goat horns on top of its head, like this. Each horn should form a pointed tip.

STEP 17

When you're happy with the horns, use black and white blocks to create its eerie eyes. At this point you can add more black blocks to its head. Its eyes sit on the border of the two colours.

Check out those brilliant horns!

STEP 18

Now turn to the back of the torso. Add a layer of green blocks as the base for the snake tail.

View from the back

STEP 19

Create the snake tail using the green blocks. It should curl and twist like a slippery snake. Take a look at the bottom picture to help you get the snake shape just how you want it.

STEP 20

Adding a layer of yellow blocks to the underside of the snake is super effective. This makes it look like a serpent belly. Don't fancy yellow? Try a different colour!

STEP 21

Be sure that your snake tail blends into the rest of your build. Add a layer of green and yellow blocks to its belly. This is how it should look from underneath.

Back legs

STEP 22

Next create a head for the snake by building up the green blocks.

Snake head from above

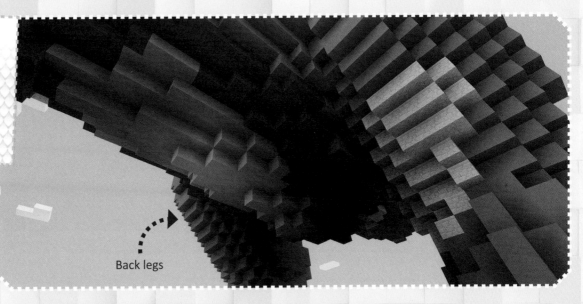

STEP 23

You're going to need lots of green blocks when it comes to getting the round face just right. The below picture shows you what it should look like from the front.

STEP 24

Build out its top jaw so that it looks something like this from the side. This is a good time to give the snake a nose shape, too. Have a go!

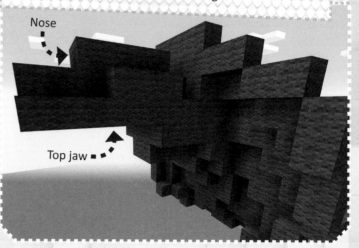

Nose

Top jaw

STEP 25

Give the snake a bottom jaw. We've built ours to have a wide open mouth. Check it out! The bottom jaw should go down in steps.

STEP 26

Add some cool highlights to its face with lighter green blocks. It works well if the light green follows the lower jawline, plus any other areas you want to stand out!

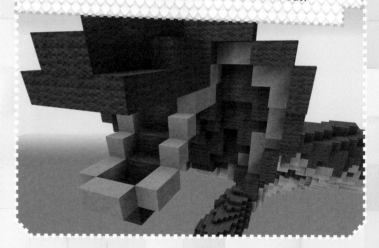

STEP 27

We've added a layer of yellow and green blocks all the way along its underbelly so that it reaches its chin. Use the brightest green blocks for its eyes, then give it some deadly white fags! Your monster should now be looking totally awesome, so go and show it off to your mates.

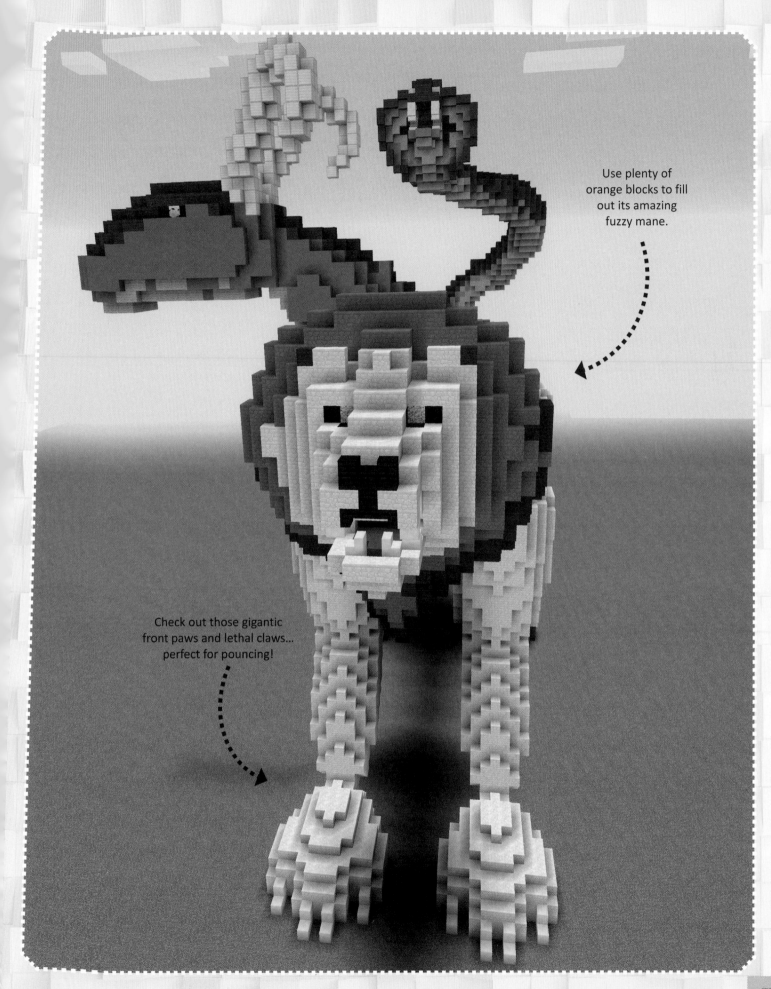

Use plenty of orange blocks to fill out its amazing fuzzy mane.

Check out those gigantic front paws and lethal claws... perfect for pouncing!

GLOSSARY

DEVOUR
To eat something quickly

DWELLING
A place to live, such as a house or an area in nature such as a river

FOLKLORE
Stories passed down through generations, often shaping the beliefs and traditions of a community

HAVOC
Causing damage and destruction

HEADDRESS
Decorative covering or band for the head, sometimes worn for ceremonies

HERALDRY
Design, study and regulation of armour

HUMANOID
Creatures that aren't human, despite looking very similar to one

LETHAL
Something that is harmful, destructive or deadly!

MEAD HALL
Gathering places for the warriors of Anglo-Saxon culture

MYTH
Traditional stories which often involve the supernatural and are told to explain a phenomenon

NIMBLE
Thinking or moving in a way that is quick and accurate

NORSE
An old word for the people of Scandinavia

RIVER STYX
Dividing river that separates the land of the living and the underworld in Greek mythology

SCANDINAVIAN
A group of people living in countries in northern Europe, including Denmark, Norway and Sweden.

SHOWDOWN
Confrontation or battle between two or more people or groups

TEMPLE
Building specifically for religious or spiritual rituals and activities such as prayer

TOMB
Large vault used for burying the dead

TORSO
The trunk part of the body that doesn't include the legs, arms or head